# the Garfield Gallery

## Gallery 4

### Jim Davis

**HODDER AND STOUGHTON**
LONDON SYDNEY AUCKLAND TORONTO

British Library Cataloguing in Publication Data

Davis, Jim, *1945—*
    The Garfield gallery 4
    1. American wit and humour, Pictorial
    I. Title
    741.5'973      NC1429

    ISBN 0-340-39792-6

First published in Great Britain 1986
Second impression 1987

Published by Hodder and Stoughton Children's Books,
a division of Hodder and Stoughton Ltd,
Mill Road, Dunton Green, Sevenoaks, Kent TN13 2YJ

Printed in Italy by New Interlitho S.p.A., Milan

TOUCH MY FOOD AND YOU'RE ONE DEAD DOG

JIM DAVIS

7-11

We shall start
no work
before it's nine

The Buck Stops Here!

JIM DAVIS

I need a
little push
now and then